MARK
TULLY

RAM CHANDER'S STORY

D1623046

PENGUIN BOOKS

PENGUIN BOOKS

Published by the Penguin Group. Penguin Books Ltd, 27 Wrights Lane, London
w8 5tz, England. Penguin Books USA Inc., 375 Hudson Street, New York, New
York 10014, USA. Penguin Books Australia Ltd, Ringwood, Victoria, Australia.
Penguin Books Canada Ltd, 10 Alcorn Avenue, Toronto, Ontario, Canada m4v 3b2.
Penguin Books (NZ) Ltd, 182–190 Wairau Road, Auckland 10, New Zealand ·
Penguin Books Ltd, Registered Offices: Harmondsworth, Middlesex, England ·
**This extract is taken from *No Full Stops in India* by Mark Tully, published
by Penguin Books in 1992.** This edition published 1995 · Copyright © Mark
Tully, 1991. All rights reserved · The moral right of the author has been asserted ·
Typeset by Datix International Limited, Bungay, Suffolk. Printed in England by
Clays Ltd, St Ives plc · Except in the United States of America, this book is sold
subject to the condition that it shall not, by way of trade or otherwise, be lent, re-
sold, hired out, or otherwise circulated without the publisher's prior consent in any
form of binding or cover other than that in which it is published and without a
similar condition including this condition being imposed on the subsequent pur-
chaser · 10 9 8 7 6 5 4 3 2 1

Bed tea or chota hazari (small breakfast), as we used to know it when I was a child in Calcutta during the last days of the raj, is one of the luxuries of my life in India. It's one I would be able to appreciate more if I had the self-discipline not to drink until eleven o'clock or so at night, eat a vast dinner and then go straight to bed, even though I know my digestion will only just be starting to cope with such excesses when the time comes for me to get up. Waking up would be easier if I had a more old-fashioned servant: some of those who lived here during the raj have admitted that they knew it was time to get up when they felt their cheek and realized they had been shaved. My Ram Chander's banging on the door is not much more kindly than the hammering of the corporal's baton at the end of my bed when I was in the army.

Ram Chander, or 'Chandre' as I have come to know him, is not one of those smooth, smart, silent, servants of the raj. He would stand, if he ever stood straight, about five foot four. He doesn't stoop, but he always seems to lean – perhaps because anything akin to a straight line is abhorrent to him. No amount of encouragement will make him eat three meals a day, so he is thin almost to the point of emaciation. He caught smallpox as a child, and so his face is pockmarked and one eye is covered by a glaucous film. Whatever clothes he wears become instantly crumpled, and his hair, although thinning, has a will of its own. Chandre speaks no English, for which I am to blame since I have never made any effort to teach him – in this city of snobs, I don't want to lose one of the few opportunities I get to practise my Hindi.

It would be surprising if Chandre were a Jeeves, because he comes from a caste which is not normally promoted beyond the lowest ranks of the servants' quarters – he is from the bhangi or sweeper caste, at the bottom of even the Harijan caste hierarchy. But Chandre is no upstart; the success he has made of his life has not gone to his head. I can imagine that in these egalitarian days many will regard it as the height of condescension for me to describe his becoming my servant as a success, but that is the way Chandre looks on it because he is a lot better off than most people from his village.

Condescension is a trap which anyone who writes about his servant can easily fall into. The word 'servant' itself shocks liberal consciences, but that is what Chandre is. So why do I want to write about him? One reason, of course, is because I think that I have a good story to tell. I also hope that his story will show those who have a horror of the caste system that a Harijan is a human being. Ever since Mahatma Gandhi awoke India and the world to the suffering of Harijans, they have been much pitied. But all too often those whom we pity become pitiable. Our concern, our anger about their plight, denies them humanity. Above all, I hope that I am paying a tribute to the affection that Chandre and I have for each other.

Chandre does not know the year of his birth. That's not uncommon in an Indian village, where life is still not measured exactly in ages – the ages for joining and leaving school, the legal age for marriage, or even the legal age to vote. These all exist in law, of course, but rural India has never been a great respecter of that. All that Chandre does know is that he was still a child when the jhagra or troubles took place.

The troubles – the partition riots of 1947 – found Chandre and his mother in Lahore. His mother was working as a sweeper in a lunatic asylum. Chandre told me, 'My father was not alive by then. He was a big strong man, like you, but he died about a year after I was born. He died in one minute, at night.' Chandre did not know what had happened in that minute.

I asked Chandre what he remembered of the bloodshed in Lahore. He replied with his usual brevity, 'Much rioting.'

Lahore, the magnificent capital of Punjab, became part of Pakistan after partition, and Hindus like Chandre's mother fled to Delhi. No one knows exactly how many fled or how many Muslims tried to make their way to Pakistan in what must surely have been one of the greatest upheavals of history. About half a million people were killed, many of them butchered in trains. Chandre and his mother were lucky. He remembers that the train journey from Lahore to Delhi, a distance of about 300 miles, took several days. He also remembers a mob stopping the train.

'On the way, near the start of the journey, someone attacked the train. I don't know who. The carriage was

3

crowded, great big men were weeping, we were all scared. We shut all the windows and doors, and I hid under a seat. Then the military came and we reached Delhi safely.'

After that adventurous beginning to his life, Chandre could well have just settled down to being one of millions of Harijans working on the land in Uttar Pradesh, India's most populous state. His village is Molanpur, post office Gavvan – a villager always describes his home by his local post office – district Badayun. It is about four hours' drive from Delhi. Chandre's family was better off than most Harijans because they did own some land. According to Chandre, his grandfather had at least ninety bighas (fifteen acres) but he lost a lot of that to the Ganges, which meanders where it likes through the soft soil. His uncle was still farming about fifty bighas when Chandre was a boy, grazing the buffaloes and goats. His mother used to make ghi, or clarified butter, from the buffaloes' milk and sell it in the bazaar at Gavvan, only a mile away by foot. As soon as he was strong enough, Chandre was taught to plough with bullocks. Then he worked the year round in the fields – sometimes his family's and sometimes other people's which his family had taken as share-croppers, sharing the produce with the owners on a fifty-fifty basis.

Chandre was perfectly happy. 'Farm work goes on twelve months of the year. We lived well and I was never hungry.'

'What about school?' I asked Chandre when I was trying to piece together the story of his childhood.

'There was no school in my village. I learnt to read from my own children.'

There was actually a school, I discovered later, but it

didn't teach much which seemed relevant to working on the land, and Chandre had no other ambitions at that time.

'If life was satisfactory for you, how did you come to Delhi?' I asked.

'Oh, that was because of the big row.'

I imagined there had been some massive dispute over land which had driven Chandre out of his village. But not at all – it was a sudden storm, although it must have been brewing for some time.

'I left home because I argued with my mother. She told me to go, otherwise why should I go?'

'But why did your mother tell you to go?'

'Because she got angry with me.'

'There must have been some reason for her getting angry with you.'

'I suppose there was. I did have a bad temper.'

'So you lost your temper.'

'No, not me – my mother.'

Extracting information from Chandre was trying my patience so I said rather irritably, 'Chandre, I don't understand. What was the row about? Surely your mother didn't just get angry for no reason at all.'

That at last got Chandre going. 'Well no. One evening I returned home to find the buffaloes and bullocks lowing because they hadn't been fed. I said that my cousin should give the buffaloes green fodder. I said that I spent the whole day working in the fields and what I brought home everyone ate, so why couldn't my cousin at least look after the animals and give the fodder. My mother said, "If you leave the house there'll be no fighting." That night I was sleeping in the fields while the maize was growing, to keep away the wild animals. In the field I thought, "My mother has never spoken to me like this in the whole of my life and so I should go." I left the next morning from the fields and no one knew that I had gone. No one knew where I had gone. I had eighty rupees with me and the clothes I was wearing.'

It is quite possible that Chandre would have cooled down and returned to his village to make peace with his mother had he not met a member of his biradari or subcaste on the road – described by Chandre as one of his relatives. Chandre has an army of so-called relatives, who are always demanding his attendance at weddings, funerals or other family occasions. He asked Chandre where he was going, and Chandre replied without thinking, 'To find work.'

His relative said, 'But you have work in your village and you have land, so why do you want to go outside.'

Then Chandre told him the story about his mother. His relative replied, 'Your mother should not have spoken like that. You have done right. You can come with me – I have work in Delhi.'

So Chandre arrived in the capital of India with just the clothes he was standing up in and his eighty rupees. His relative was living in what is known as a jhuggi-jhonpri, that is a cluster of one-roomed shacks normally consisting of mud walls and rusty corrugated-iron roofs. Even someone as short as Chandre could not stand up inside the jhuggi. The jhuggi-jhonpri had sprung up on the edge of a construction site because, as usual, the contractors had made no attempt to house the migrant labourers building in this case a hospital. Chandre's relative was working as a labourer, carrying sand and bricks on his head.

The next day, Chandre's relative sent him off to buy atta or flour for making chapattis, but Chandre was never to return. It wasn't that he didn't want to return – he had nowhere else to go and was very grateful to his relative – but he just got lost. When I asked Chandre how he could have got lost when there must have been plenty of atta shops nearby and plenty of people to ask the way back to the construction site, Chandre replied, 'I crossed the road to the shop, bought the atta and then forgot the way.'

'But it must have been a big construction site. Some people must have known the way back to it,' I said.

'Yes, it was a big site, but I didn't know what to ask for. I had only arrived the night before, so I didn't know. I wandered around all day and in the evening I found myself in Akbar Road.' Akbar Road is one of the tree-lined avenues of the original New Delhi. Its colonial bungalows set in large gardens are occupied by ministers, senior civil servants and service officers. Chandre must have walked a long way from north Delhi to get to this, the most sought-after part of the capital. The burra sahibs of independent India live like their colonial predecessors in an artificially sanitized zone, removed from all the discomforts suffered by the people they are governing or administering. Chandre was overcome by the alien orderliness of it all.

'There were no people on the streets, no shops. So I finally realized that I was completely lost and there was no one to ask. It was getting dark, I had nowhere to go, so I just sat down by a rubbish heap and started to cry. I couldn't think of anything else to do.'

'Did you spend the night on the streets?' I asked.

'No. You remember our dhobi [washerman], Sohan Lal? A friend of his came by and asked me why I was crying. He said, "Don't worry. Come with me," and that night he gave me food and a place to sleep. He asked me my caste and I said I was a bhangi. But he didn't mind. He was a dhobi.'

'Did you feel uneasy because you were a sweeper, not from their caste?'

'No, there was nothing like that. I didn't feel like that. I spoke to Sohan Lal and his family and they didn't let me feel anything.'

I was a little surprised by this, so I said, 'Sohan Lal's family had absolutely no reason for taking you in. You were not related. They didn't know your family. They didn't come from the same area.'

'No, they just felt sorry for me when I told them that I had arrived in Delhi the night before, had been told to go and buy atta and had got lost. They said, "You stay here until you find your relative, otherwise you will die."'

Chandre could well have died or got lost in the underworld of Delhi if Sohan Lal's family had not taken pity on him. To this day, Chandre remains a very nervous traveller. Recently he was sent by train to Allahabad to meet me. Before I left, I assured him that the Prayagraj Express terminated at Allahabad, but a tired Chandre told me he had sat up all night in case he missed the station.

Sohan Lal's family lived in the servants' quarters at the back of a large compound in Akbar Road. A senior naval officer called Nayar was living in the bungalow – he must have been an admiral to qualify for such spacious accommodation. Chandre was taken to see Nayar Sahib the next morning. Nayar telephoned a friend who was looking for a sweeper and suggested that he took on Chandre. But Chandre once again failed to reach his destination.

'Nayar Sahib's sweeper told me to go behind the Ashoka Hotel where I would find a house and to ask there about the job. There was no house – just a big hotel – so I wandered round all day and then luckily found my way back to Nayar Sahib's house in the evening.'

'What did Nayar Sahib say?'

'He called the dhobi and asked him whether I got the job. The dhobi told him that there was no house where the sweeper had sent me. So the sahib called in the sweeper and asked him why he had told me to go to the wrong place. The sweeper said he had gone for the job himself – I suppose it was better paid. Anyhow, Nayar Sahib got very angry with the sweeper and said, "This man will work here now."'

Chandre worked for Nayar Sahib for five years – or at least that is as he remembers it: I am a little doubtful whether a senior naval officer would have remained in one posting for so long. Anyhow, it was during Nayar Sahib's time that Chandre met and married his wife. Under normal circumstances Chandre's marriage would have been arranged for him by his family and the biradari or subcaste, but he had 9 not had any contact with his village since he had arrived in Delhi. So it was that Nayar Sahib acted as the head of Chandre's biradari – or perhaps it would be more accurate to say his marriage-broker. It all happened very suddenly, as Chandre explained in his laconic way.

'A man was running off with a girl in Nayar Sahib's time. He came to the compound where I lived. We were all on duty, so the women asked him who he was, where he had come from, what caste he was. He got frightened and ran away. Perhaps the police were after him. He left the girl behind and didn't come back. Then, after some days, all the compound people – the dudh-wallah [milkman], the mali [gardener], the dhobi and all the rest of them – went to the sahib. He called the girl. She told him she had no relatives in Delhi and was not married. The compound-wallahs suggested the marriage. The sahib asked if she wanted to stay with me. So it was fixed.'

'Did the sahib ask you whether you wanted to marry the girl?'

'I can't remember. The sahib took us to a navy place in his car where we had an official marriage and put our thumb-prints on the papers.'

Chandre did not bother to find out about the man who had brought his wife to the compound.

'I never asked my wife. She didn't tell me either. Later her mother did say that a man used to come to their house, but they didn't know who he was. It appeared to be something about love. My wife was very beautiful.'

'What about her caste?'

'She told Nayar Sahib she was a sweeper, so I took her to belong to the same caste as I did.'

Neither Chandre nor his new wife made any attempt to contact her family. That, like most things in Chandre's life, happened by accident. One day the newly-weds were together in a market near Akbar Road when they were spotted by his wife's sister-in-law, who worked there. She ran up to Parvati, Chandre's wife, and asked her what she was doing with a man. Parvati explained that she was now married, and so the sister-in-law took the couple to the hospital where Parvati's parents were working. They were, according to Chandre, 'happy at the marriage'. But Chandre still did not tell his own family and biradari.

Eventually the inevitable happened and Nayar Sahib was posted. A new Anglo-Indian naval officer took over the bungalow in Akbar Road. He was, according to Chandre, a little more inquisitive.

'I never used to go back to my village like the other servants do. One day the new sahib asked me why I didn't. He then asked me about my village, its name, the name of the post office, the name of the tehsil [revenue area] and district. Then he sent a letter to my mother. She came to Delhi and we met again. For five years I had not seen anyone from my village.'

I asked Chandre what he had felt when he first saw his mother after so many years. He shook his head slowly and said, '*Kuch nahin*' – 'Nothing.'

'After all those years, nothing?'

'Nothing, I suppose,' he said.

Nevertheless, Chandre was apparently glad to re-establish his connections with his village because he started going home again. There inevitably he came under pressure from his relatives to find jobs in the big city for them too. To demonstrate his status as a man of the world, he gave the job in Akbar Road to his sister's husband and moved on to a guest-house where he was the sweeper for three or four sahibs. When they left, all the staff lost their jobs and the cook and Chandre set off to find work as a team. They worked together for three years and then the cook introduced Chandre to one of his relatives – Garib Prasad, a long-serving BBC cook. It was through Garib Prasad that Chandre first came to work for me. Neither of us can remember the year exactly, but it must have been about 1972.

At that stage in my family's life the household was dominated by Garib and his wife, who somehow managed to look after my children as well as her own seven. The Garibs were part of our family, and Chandre did not, I am ashamed to say, impinge on our lives very much. Garib belonged to the old school of servants who believed that the cook was the boss. What is more, he did not really approve of Chandre's frequent absences in his village – absences which were always extended well beyond the day he had promised to return. Eventually Garib decided that we must have a sweeper who could be relied on, and Chandre returned to his village for good – or at least that was what he thought. He was quite happy about that, because there was no one to look after the land. There was another reason for Chandre's return to the village. It was in his words the '*aurat ka chakkar*' or 'trouble with the woman'.

Chandre was not shocked when I asked whether that meant that his wife was involved with another man or that he was involved with another woman. He smiled and said, 'It does happen sometimes in the village – you can't do anything about it – but it wasn't that trouble. I told you that my wife was very fair. But she also suffered very badly from fits. She had them very often.'

'So you went back to look after her.'

'Yes. That was why I kept on taking a holiday from you, and in the end Garib said I would have to go, so I did.'

By this time Chandre had a daughter, Rani, and a son, Mahesh. After Chandre's return, his wife bore him another son. He died soon after birth, and Chandre's wife died two or three days later.

Chandre stayed in the village until his son, Mahesh, fell ill. He then returned to Delhi to stay with his sister and get treatment for Mahesh. He managed to get a job cleaning some offices and re-established his contacts with the domestic servants' circle. That, he explained, was how he came back to my house.

'Garib was ill in the Mool Chand Hospital near where you were living then. He called for me and said that I should join him again, because he had not found a sweeper he could work with. So I came back.'

Neither my wife – Margaret – nor I knew about all those machinations, but we were very happy to have Chandre back again. In so far as he ever showed any emotion at that stage in our relationship, Chandre seemed to be reasonably pleased too.

Two years later Garib died. We were all heartbroken – especially my children. Garib had been with us since we first came to India, fifteen years earlier. None of us could imagine an outsider in Garib's kitchen, so we hit on the idea of Chandre – who was by now very much an insider. When Margaret put this to Chandre, he turned it down flat. He said, 'I can't do it, because I am not a good enough cook.'

Margaret tried to persuade him. 'You have been working with Garib and other cooks for so long you must have learnt something about cooking.'

'No. I am a sweeper, and I am very happy. I would not like to let you down or to make you angry with me because the food was not good.'

Margaret refused to give up. 'Come on, Chandre,' she said. 'I have seen you cooking sometimes. When Garib was tired he used to sit on the chair and tell you what to do.'

'Yes, but Garib isn't here to tell me what to do now,' said Chandre with flawless logic.

'I will teach you,' offered Margaret.

But Chandre had an answer to that one: 'It would not be proper for you to spend your time in the kitchen.'

Margaret knew how stubborn Chandre could be, so she decided to leave it for the moment, saying, 'Well, Chandre, I don't know what we can do, because all the children say they won't have anyone else.'

The matter was left for a few days, during which Margaret and our daughters did the cooking – much to Chandre's horror: he had never seen a memsahib working in the kitchen except when there was something really special to be cooked.

Garib's death left us with the problem of his family too. His eldest son was now in a good job with an advertising agency, but the rest of the family still had to be looked after. What was worse, if we took on another cook he would have demanded Garib's quarters and there would have been nowhere for the family to go. We discussed this problem with Garib's eldest son, and he came up with an answer which has worked to everyone's total satisfaction ever since. He suggested that Mamaji, as we all knew Garib's wife, should work in the kitchen with Chandre. That would give her an income, and something to take her mind off the loss of her husband. Sham Lal, Garib's son, didn't see any problem in his mother working with a sweeper as cook, and promised to put the idea to her when he felt she was sufficiently recovered. He soon managed to persuade her, on condition that Chandre handled the cookbook – that accounting horror left over from the raj. Chandre had an apparently irrefutable answer to that one: 'I can't read and write well enough to do the cookbook. I never went to school.'

Margaret agreed that she would do the cookbook, and Chandre, seeing that we were all utterly determined to get him in the kitchen, agreed to serve an apprenticeship under Mamaji. It soon became apparent that Chandre knew much more about cooking than he had admitted. It also emerged that Chandre was not totally illiterate, and after a few months he took charge of the cookbook too.

It is now ten years since Garib died and Chandre took

over. Margaret and I are separated – a matter of great sadness to Chandre and Mamaji, but they get on very well with Gilly who lives with me. Chandre's style is very unorthodox, but I wouldn't change him for the best-trained servant in India, and his cooking is superb.

Chandre, like all good servants, is the real ruler of the house. If I go to sleep again after his early-morning knock, he'll say, 'I thought you had a lot to drink last night.' In the evening, he gives me an old-fashioned look if I move on from beer to whisky. Chandre won't allow me to serve drinks to my guests: he says, 'Sahib, I am the servant in this house and this is my job.' Towards the end of the evening he sometimes comes and joins in the conversation, leaning on a bookcase which divides the room. He doesn't say much unless the conversation turns to religion, as it does from time to time. Then he will often express his certainty that there is a god up there. Chandre controls my eating as well as my drinking. As soon as breakfast is over he'll insist on knowing what's wanted for lunch, and as soon as that's over I have to turn my attention to dinner. He is in charge of the cookbook, and nothing comes before keeping that up to date and in funds. Chandre doesn't have it all his own way – Mrs Garib gives as good as she gets in the kitchen – but basically Chandre is the boss.

He's at his most imperious when keeping unwanted guests away. In India, a man's home is very much not his castle: everyone feels free to call at all times. I much prefer this to the nuclear family and the formality of Britain, but there are times when I have seen enough of someone – or indeed of everyone. Then Chandre comes into his own, lying with the utmost conviction to keep unwanted intruders out. There was, for instance, the occasion when the car was parked around the corner and all the lights were off in the flat downstairs, to give the impression we were out. We were actually sitting watching television upstairs in the office. Even upstairs we heard the impatient hammering on the front door, but we weren't worried because we were sure Chandre would deal with the intruders. A few minutes later Chandre came upstairs, looking slightly unsure of himself.

'Sahib, when I went to the door I found a lot of people in khaki with guns. I thought the police had come, so I was very worried and I thought of shutting the door. Then I thought, supposing they get annoyed? We don't want to get taken to the police station. So I came to ask you what to do.'

I couldn't think of any reason for the police to come to get me, but in India it's always best to stay on the right side of the law so I told Chandre to go down and ask them whether their business couldn't wait until tomorrow because I was very busy broadcasting to London. I find that this is usually quite an effective excuse. Chandre was soon back again for more advice.

'Sahib, I can't tell them to go away,' he said. 'They are the security guards for Chaudhuri Devi Lal – he has come to see you.'

I agreed with Chandre that we could not turn the redoubtable chaudhuri, or headman, away, and so I went down to welcome him and apologize for the delay.

Chaudhuri Devi Lal was then the chief minister of Haryana

and was soon to become the deputy prime minister. At seventy-five, he is the patriarch of the Jats, the Indian farming caste which dominates the villages surrounding Delhi. Some six feet two inches tall, broadly built, with a good head of white hair and a deep gravelly voice, he is every inch a leader. The chaudhuri is hated by the élite because he is proud of his rural background and makes no pretence to the sort of sophistication they admire.

Chandre always remembers another occasion when Chaudhuri Sahib came to call. This time it was breakfast. Chandre had laid on what we all thought would please the chaudhuri's rustic tastes – egg brujia (a sort of spiced scrambled egg), a vegetable curry, lassi (liquefied curd) and crisply fried parathas. All seemed to go well until Chaudhuri Sahib said to Gilly, 'These are very good parathas. What oil do you use?'

'Groundnut oil,' replied Gilly.

The chaudhuri hurriedly dropped his half-eaten paratha. In a shocked tone he said, 'You don't use ghi.' Then, realizing that he had to provide some excuse for not finishing his meal, he said, 'You know, my doctor has told me to restrict my diet.' In towns ghi is considered a luxury, but to a self-respecting farmer it's the only acceptable cooking medium.

Devi Lal never came to breakfast again, but this hasn't spoilt our friendship, though Chandre is disappointed that the chaudhuri didn't find time to come to the house after becoming deputy prime minister.

Chandre really comes into his own when there is a big party and we have to call in outside caterers. Then he regards it as his job to see that the bearers don't get drunk or remove too many bottles for themselves. Chandre can also produce a meal under the most adverse circumstances. Corbett Park, the national park just below the foothills of the Himalayas, is better known for its tigers than for its cuisine. We take Chandre with us whenever we go, because even without a kitchen his performance far outstrips that of the cooks working for the contractor who runs the café there. One evening, after he had reluctantly been for an elephant ride and seen a tiger, Chandre was crouched over a kerosene stove outside our quarters. Suddenly the pots behind him clattered. Chandre turned, saw two green eyes staring at him in the semi-darkness and ran inside. When we came back we found the cooking pots all higgledy-piggledy, our dinner spilt on the floor and no sign of Chandre. We shouted for him and he came out looking shaken. 'Sahib, a tiger came,' he said. 'I saw his eyes. So I ran.'

My son Pat was not convinced, and said, 'Chandre, if a tiger came into this compound there would have been a hell of a hangama [uproar]. There are so many people here. They would have seen it.'

But Chandre insisted that it was a tiger. Pat, who was tired after a day in the jungle, went into his room and threw himself on to his bed. There was a sharp hiss and Chandre's tiger shot out of the door. Chandre had got the family right, but not the species – it was a scruffy domestic, but not domesticated, cat.

We Europeans always like to impose our ideas on our servants: we feel we are doing them good and, of course, at the same time storing up merit for ourselves. It was inevitable, therefore, that we should all concern ourselves with the education of Chandre's son, Mahesh. Arrangements were made to get him enrolled in the best government school in the locality, and off he went. No one thought much more about this until one day I saw Mahesh pedalling one of the cycle-rickshaws which ply between the main road outside our house and the railway station. This was now not a question of some vague merit we hoped to earn, it was much more serious than that – the izzat or honour of the household was at stake. I rushed inside and called Chandre.

'What the hell is Mahesh doing pulling that rickshaw?'

Chandre looked rather sheepish and said, 'I can't get him to stay at school and so he has decided to earn his living. He says that he can't hear and then the master beats him.'

'What do you mean can't hear?'

'He says that he has some trouble with his ears. I have been to see the master and he refuses to have Mahesh back. He said, "I don't want a boy like that in my school."'

'Well, for God's sake get him off that damn rickshaw!'

Mahesh didn't seem too unhappy to be forbidden to pull a rickshaw, which is very hard work indeed. The next step was to get him to a doctor. This we did without too much difficulty, but when an operation for his ears was suggested Mahesh once again flatly refused to cooperate. He said he would rather die than go into hospital. So that seemed to rule out education. The next best thing was some sort of training. Fortunately Babu Lal, one of the mechanics who run an open-air car-repair business on the taxi rank opposite us, agreed to take on Mahesh. I have to say that his attendance there is not much more regular than his attendance at school, but Babu Lal is more tolerant than the master. Obviously you can take Mahesh to water but you can't make him drink. My only consolation is that he did learn to read and write before getting himself expelled from school.

It does not redound to my credit that it was many years before I visited Chandre's village, although it's only about four hours' drive from Delhi. Chandre is very proud of his village and of its temple, but somehow I had never found time to go there. Then one day Chandre came into my office and said, 'Sahib, can I have a loan of 20,000 rupees?' I was somewhat taken aback, because Chandre's personal and family problems had usually been solved with smaller sums. When I asked why he wanted this large loan, Chandre looked sheepish and said, '*Rani ki shadi*' – 'For Rani's wedding.'

I knew that Chandre's daughter, Rani, was only about sixteen, and that we were all meant to be encouraging late marriages to help with family planning and the emancipation of women. But I also knew that once Chandre had made up his mind there was no point in arguing. So I said to him, 'I hope you have found a good boy for Rani. She is a very good girl.'

'Yes,' replied Chandre. 'When I was in my village, the chaudhuri of our biradari came to see me. He is an old friend. He asked whether I would like him to fix a boy for my daughter. I said yes, but I didn't hear anything for six or seven months. Then the chaudhuri came to me and suggested that I should agree to give Rani to one of his relatives.' He   21 explained the relationship by saying that the chaudhuri's son would be Rani's '*nand ka devar*' when she married. After drawing several family trees, I came to the conclusion that Rani's fiancé was the chaudhuri's son's wife's younger brother. Relationships in northern India are very complicated to unravel, because there is a separate word for each relative. It's not, for example, good enough to say 'cousin': you have to know the word which means 'my elder maternal uncle's son'.

After we had sorted out that little problem, Chandre went on to tell me that the rishta, or proposal, had already been formally accepted. 'In our biradari,' he said, 'we from the girl's side have to go to the boy's village. There we take the rishta and it is formally accepted. I went with fourteen people including Mahesh. Twelve came from Delhi, two from the village. I had to take with me sweets, fruit and 150 rupees in cash to give to the boy's family. They gave us a feast and so the rishta was pukka.'

'Was that all you gave?' I asked.

'Oh no. I had to take the suit length for the boy of terry cotton, shoes, a shirt and a gold ring. I had to take five kurta pajamas [loose-fitting tunics and trousers] for the boy's father and uncles, and five saris for the ladies of the family. It cost about 4,000 rupees.'

'But you didn't want a loan at that stage?'

'No, I have some money saved up in a drawer in the house.'

'In this house!' I said angrily. 'You know we have had three burglaries.'

'It's locked in a drawer downstairs. The burglar only steals from the office upstairs,' replied Chandre with perfect logic.

'Why on earth don't you use a bank? It'll be much safer, and you may get interest.'

'No, I don't trust banks. You may have to pay a bribe to get the money out. Many people have told me that.'

Bribes are usually only paid to get loans, but I gave up and asked Chandre whether Rani's fiancé was literate. Gilly and Avrille, who works in our office, had told Chandre a hundred times to make sure he married Rani to a well-educated boy who could get a good job. But Chandre hadn't bothered to find out what his future son-in-law's educational achievements were. They turned out to be minimal. Chandre insisted it would all be all right, because he knew the family well, but it wasn't until after the marriage that he learnt that the boy's father had two wives and innumerable children.

Chandre's biradari has not yet been corrupted by the middle-class practice of giving dowries, and so he was not presented with a long list of goods which he would have to provide in order to get his daughter married. Nevertheless, Chandre himself drew up a fairly formidable list of gifts to give to the couple. It was, quite naturally, a question of izzat or self-respect for Chandre to show that he was able to provide for his daughter properly. This was Chandre's list:

one television set,
one scooter,
thirty-one degchis (handleless saucepans) and other cooking pots
    and pans,

thirty-one saris for the women and
seven kurta pajamas for men of the boy's family,
five saris and five silver ornaments for Rani,
one tin trunk,
one wall clock,
one wristwatch for the boy,
two chairs,
one table,
one sofa,
one bed with bedding
2,500 rupees cash.

Total value: 80,000 rupees.

When Chandre asked for the loan, I had no idea that he
would be incurring so much expenditure – I grandiosely
thought that I would be financing most of the wedding. It
never, for instance, occurred to me that Chandre would
provide a scooter for his son-in-law, because I had never seen
any of Chandre's relatives riding one. But, as the day of the
wedding drew near, the extent of Chandre's commitments
became clear as the back room of our house started to fill up
with all the gifts. I thought that I should step up my
contribution, but Chandre said, 'No. All I want you to do is
to come to the wedding, even though it is in my village and it
will not be very comfortable for you.' That was how I came
to pay my first visit to village Molanpur in Uttar Pradesh.

Gilly, Avrille and I set off for Molanpur on the day of the
wedding – a day that had been selected as auspicious by
Nirottam, a Brahmin living on the embankment at the back

of the village. We met up with Satish Jacob, my long-standing colleague in the office, at a dhaba or roadside eating-house owned by a pehlvan, or wrestler, in Gajraula, a small town on the main road from Delhi to Lucknow. There is a whole host of dhabas there because long-distance buses from Delhi stop to allow their passengers to eat. The competition is stiff so the food is good, but the pleasure of eating it is somewhat reduced by the highly offensive odour from a chemical factory on the edge of the town. The leaves on the trees were shrivelled – presumably due to pollution from the factory – and I did wonder what chemicals had penetrated the wrestler's food, but we were all hungry and so I didn't raise that question.

Rattan Singh, the retired wrestler, was sitting cross-legged on a charpai, his face unshaven, his eyes hidden behind dark glasses. He said very little – his presence was enough to ensure the smooth flow of food in his dhaba. He was once the champion of northern India, but he had retired several years ago. The surrogates he now employed to fight for him were strutting around wire cages outside the dhaba. They had swollen red combs instead of cauliflower ears, and battered beaks instead of broken noses. They were better-fed than the guests at his dhaba, getting regular meals of raisins and almonds. Rattan Singh assured me that his fighting cocks were just as formidable as he'd once been.

After we had joined up with Satish and eaten our lunch, we turned off the national highway to Lucknow and drove along the road to Gavvan, the town near Chandre's village. It was April – one of the hottest months of the year. The brain-fever bird's cry rose higher and higher up the scale as it screeched, 'It's getting hotter, it's getting hotter, and I can't *stand* it, can't *stand* it, can't *stand* it.' I thought I would get brain-fever too if I didn't stop our little red van and take a break in one of the cool, green mango groves which flanked the road, but we were late – as always – and couldn't disappoint Chandre.

We passed through the town of Hasanpur, where white-capped Muslims lounged in the shade of mosque courtyards waiting for the evening prayers and the break in the fast of Ramzan, the Muslim month of fasting. In the centre of the town a fine old family house built around a cool courtyard still survived. Much of its plasterwork was intact, but the finely carved wooden balconies were collapsing and the whole place had an ill-kempt air about it. Clearly it was soon to fall victim to the greed of the contractors, who were just waiting to complete the transformation of Hasanpur into yet another hot and ugly concrete cauldron.

Leaving the town, we passed two immaculate white bullocks shaking their heads in unison as they laboured under the yoke of a cart carrying vegetables to market. In the countryside, horse-drawn traps or tongas and bullock carts have still not totally surrendered to three-wheeled phut-phuts of all shapes and sizes emitting all forms of pollution. At first the land was quite fertile. Shisham trees lined the roads, and young sugar cane sprouted in the fields. On the bank of one field we saw a black redstart, his tail quivering energetically. He too was apparently suffering from brain fever, because by now he should have been on his way up to the Himalayas. As we went on, the land became more barren – wild charas or cannabis grew in the scrub, the bushes were stunted, the date-palms had been mutilated by villagers always short of fodder for their goats and cattle. The earth was dusty and white – the sort of soil that makes me feel hot just to look at it. What agriculture there was seemed comparatively primitive. We passed two more bullocks, this time plodding round and round in circles turning a Persian wheel – a form of irrigation which has been replaced by electric and diesel pumps in the more prosperous areas of northern India.

Eventually we reached Gavvan, where Rani's wedding had been arranged. As we drove in to the town, we were flagged down by an anxious Chandre who had been here since the morning. He had apparently forgotten that I'd told him we'd be lunching in Gajraula. Knowing Chandre's deficient sense of direction, I was relieved to be told that he'd brought one of his young relatives to ride ahead of the van on a scooter and lead us to the village.

We drove through the town, paid a two-rupee toll to cross a bridge and then turned right down an even narrower road. The area around the village was more productive than the scrubland we had just passed through. This was the season for sunflower as well as arabi, a root crop with leaves like elephant ears. One field was guarded by a scrawny scarecrow. The tarmac soon gave out and we bucked and reared along a mud track leading to Molanpur, the scooter-rider performing miraculous feats of balance to remain wheelborne. Eventually we came to the village, but we didn't stop. We passed the village pond, with the inevitable black buffaloes wallowing 27 peacefully in it, and drove on until we came to a cluster of mud houses – Chandre's basti. Harijan bastis, or settlements, are always on the outskirts of villages.

There were six thatched houses with mud walls built around an open space of about eighty by seventy feet. More houses were built off the courtyard facing the track, which led in one direction to the main part of the village and in the other direction to the embankment protecting Molanpur and its lands from the Ganges. I had expected that we would be surrounded by curious villagers as soon as we stopped, but everyone was far too busy with preparations for the wedding to bother about us. Chandre got out and led us into the courtyard, where he showed us his house with a certain amount of diffidence. It had a low doorway without a door and one room in which I could just about stand up. Chandre said, 'I have had the thatch done again for the wedding, but it's not really all right for you to sleep in so I've made another arrangement.' I assured Chandre that we would be quite comfortable, but he was not convinced, as he was used to seeing me in much more luxurious circumstances.

The whole basti was decorated with strings of paper flags. Banana trees had been placed on each side of the doorway of the hut where the marriage ceremony was to take place. New mango leaves – symbols of prosperity – were strung above the doorway. The walls of all the huts and the ground of the courtyard had been covered with a fresh paste of mud and cow dung. On the walls, the paste had been worked into intricate patterns – peacocks and elephants had been moulded on to it and the women of the basti had painted animals and men fighting each other inside and outside the houses. The style was very similar to many of the tribal paintings I have seen in central India. Those are now much admired as 'folk art', but I have never heard or read of 'the art' of the Harijans of western Uttar Pradesh – I suppose because they lack the glamour of tribals.

The last-minute preparations for the arrival of the barat, the bridegroom's party, were being made. A tractor trailer carrying chairs and a generator was being unloaded outside the basti. A canvas awning was being erected on wooden poles – one of the elderly women said scornfully, 'It's not very big.' Mahipal, one of Chandre's relatives who works in our office, was washing himself under a pump. He and our dhobi had arrived by the overnight bus from Delhi.

Chandre took no part in the preparations. He seemed to assume that all would be all right in the end. His only concern was that we should live life as we were used to living it. He said, 'It's five o'clock and you haven't had any tea.' Then he insisted on sitting us down at a table complete with tablecloth and went off to brew up. An old lady with a face lined like a prune, no teeth and small, round Mahatma-Gandhi-style spectacles squatted in front of Gilly and started to massage her feet, whimpering, sighing and muttering to encourage herself. Chandre came back to ask where we had put the beer. It had been hidden in the back of the van, because I wasn't quite sure about the proprieties. Chandre doesn't drink himself, and I thought that it might be inappropriate for me to drink at the wedding. I asked tentatively, 29

'Will it really be all right for us to drink beer. Won't someone object?'

Chandre said with some annoyance, 'I have arranged everything. The whole village wants to welcome you, and I have told them that you will drink beer.'

I could have wished for a somewhat different image to precede me, but there was nothing I could do about it now. If I didn't drink beer, Chandre would, I supposed, lose face. Anyway, there was the ritual of tea to get through first.

After tea, Avrille and Gilly were taken off to see the bride. Rani was being groomed for the coming wedding. Her hair had been oiled and her limbs smeared with turmeric paste, which is said to make skin smooth and fair. She was wearing an old sari borrowed from a relative, which made her look grown-up. In Delhi, like other young girls, she always wore a shalwar-qamiz – baggy trousers and a long shirt. The sari was an indication of her new status – of a married woman. She was an unconventionally pretty girl, with a dark complexion, prominent cheekbones and very large, bright, brown eyes. Ever since her engagement, she had glowed with confidence. Although she coyly refused to comment when asked what she thought of her fiancé, her smiles showed that she certainly had no objection to the match. Now that her wedding day had come she was still enjoying being the centre of attention, but she was tense because the great changes which lay ahead had at last dawned on her. 'Today we had a puja [act of worship],' she told Gilly and Avrille. 'The kumhar [potter] came, and we made offerings to Boorhe Babu. If you do that, then he stops you getting seep – light-brown patches on your skin. I shan't see you today, unless you come here to see me. I have to stay in this house now, because the barat may come any time.'

While I was waiting for Gilly and Avrille to come back, the cows appeared over the top of the embankment in a haze of dust. They were being driven home for the night by young boys. Then two buses drew up on the embankment and the barat emerged. I had expected Chandre to go out to greet it, but he was nowhere to be seen. The young men came first – dressed in gaudy, tight-fitting trousers, with open-necked shirts which clung to their narrow chests. They gaped and giggled at me and then walked on, some of them holding hands. The older men followed, dressed for the most part in traditional cotton kurtas. They politely ignored the strange foreigner seated at a neatly draped table solemnly sipping tea. The women had been left behind – in Chandre's biradari they don't travel with the barat. The bridegroom's party regrouped on the open ground on the other side of the courtyard, where they were served with soft drinks. Twenty-four hours of feasting had started.

I was not sure what to do next. Should I join in the festivities or should I not? I am easily embarrassed and hate sticking out like a sore thumb. Fortunately Gilly and Avrille returned quite soon, and, with my customary cowardice, I sent them off to find Chandre so that he could tell us what to do.

Chandre decided that it would be premature for us to join the other guests. 'You sit here,' he said. 'You will be more comfortable and I'll call some people to talk to you.' Chandre 31 went off and came back with about ten members of his biradari. It was getting dark, so hurricane lights were produced and Chandre brought the beer. I certainly felt like a drink, but I also wanted someone to drink with. Unfortunately Satish had left sometime earlier, since he had to get back to Delhi, and Gilly and Avrille both thought it would be most unladylike to join me. So there I was, left alone with my drink. However my embarrassment soon wore off under the influence of the lukewarm beer and the conversation.

One of the elders who came was Tau, a man of dismal countenance with a great moustache through which he filtered smoke from his hookah. 'Tau' means 'elder uncle', but he was in fact only Chandre's elder uncle's son – he'd gained the title of 'Tau' because he behaved and looked like an elder uncle. Tau offered the hookah stem to me, but I politely declined. I enjoy many Indian tastes, but the hookah has always defeated me. I nearly choked to death on one in Raja Bazaar in Rawalpindi.

Inevitably the conversation soon got round to weddings. Tau said, 'Ram Chandre is lucky. In my younger days the barat stayed until there was no food left in the basti. Nowadays they usually go after one day.'

Gilly asked, 'Do your boys and girls ever get married on their own, for love?' The women laughed, and one said, '"Love" – we don't understand the meaning of the word. These men just think we are there to do the work for them – from morning right through until we go to sleep at night they keep us at it.'

Another woman said, 'That's true, but if you have a good

man you become fond of him.' It was harder to understand the women than the men, because they rarely went out of the village and so their dialect was not affected by the Hindustani spoken in towns.

Kamal, a very intelligent younger relative of Chandre's, said, 'Only the educated people get married like that. They perhaps get to know each other in school. For us, an elopement is a great disgrace. I think that's right.'

Gilly quoted an old saying: '*Jab mian bibi razi, to kya karega kazi*' – 'When a boy and a girl agree, not even a qazi [a judge, one of whose duties is the registration of marriages] can do anything about it.'

The villagers laughed, and Kamal said, 'Han, you have said absolutely right. But then we don't encourage that sort of thing. We prefer to arrange it through our customs, because a young girl and a young boy – what do they know?'

I was reminded of the headman of a village just outside Delhi with whom I'd once discussed marriage. He'd said, 'In England you marry the women you love. In India we love the women we marry. You fall out of love after marriage. We fall in love after marriage.'

When I related the headman's views, Tau grunted: 'All this love talk! It has nothing to do with life in villages. Only those who don't know anything about how we live would talk of it.' That ended the conversation.

After a lengthy silence, during which Tau bubbled gloomily on his hookah, I attempted to get things going again by asking about changes in the life of the village. An elderly man with thick glasses, and wearing a rather grubby Gandhi cap, said, 'In my view the worst thing that has happened is that the police have started coming into the village. In the old days the police never came – we used to sort out our quarrels ourselves or with the panchayat [village council]. But nowadays people keep running to the court or the police station. They waste a lot of money, and achieve nothing. The police are not just. They always side with the richer person, so no matter how much you offer them you can't beat someone with more money.'

'But surely,' I asked, 'under the panchayat system you also suffered, because you were the poorest community and you were the sweepers.'

'Han, of course that was there,' the elderly villager replied. 'But, you see, many of our quarrels were among ourselves and we have our own panchayat in our biradari so they sort out the quarrels. Even when we had quarrels with the other castes, the leaders of the panchayat knew that the village could not do without us and that if too much injustice was done to us we would not do the necessary work. So it wasn't that injustice was always done to us. In a village in those days everyone knew their place, but so did everyone have a place.'

'Why do people go to the police now?'

'I'm not certain. I think maybe it's to do with the government. The government and the politicians are always saying they will do everything for us, and people believe this – even though they are always going to the government and getting nothing. Nowadays, you see, everyone thinks that only the government can do anything. Even if a person gets a good job, he doesn't think it's a suitable job unless he is an employee of the government. That's why everyone goes to the government for justice too, because they think only government justice is proper justice.'

Chandre walked into the courtyard, looking rather solemn. He came up to Tau and said, 'Now we must do the accounts. It'll be too late if we don't start now.' Tau, who was still sitting cross-legged on the ground, looked up at Chandre and said, 'Call them all, and I'll come.'

Now the real business of the wedding was to be done. Members of Chandre's biradari are expected to contribute to each other's daughters' weddings. Each person notes down the contribution he has made and then hopes to be reimbursed when his daughter gets married. The proceedings this time were supervised by a diminutive old man drowned by a giant yellow turban. He was the chaudhuri of the biradari. The chota chaudhuri, or small chaudhuri, who was actually very much larger than his superior, was there too. The negotiations took nearly three hours, but Chandre told me they went off without any serious argument. This seemed to be largely because of Chandre's good nature. I asked him whether everyone had paid his dues. 'No,' he said – 'but then they never do. My closest friends did, and others paid something, but I don't like to fight about money. You know how much money I have given to Hari Ram – my real brother, who works near Delhi – and you know he has never given anything back to me.'

Tau apparently never contributed to weddings but always took part in the negotiations. He had told me he earned only a pittance, and so I suggested to Chandre that he lacked the wherewithal to contribute to weddings.

Chandre replied, 'He's got money, but if he doesn't want to give back what I have given for his weddings I am not going to cause any trouble.'

When the business session was over, Chandre came back to us and said, 'You'd better come out now, because the barat procession will be arriving soon.' Gilly asked Chandre, 'But aren't you going to change to receive the barat?' He was wearing a distinctly dirty white shirt and a pair of trousers which had formed part of his uniform several years ago. Chandre ignored that question and went off to see what the caterers preparing the wedding dinner were up to.

We went out to the open space in front of the basti to join the villagers waiting for the barat. For some two hours we were continuously reassured, 'It's coming soon'; 'It's on the point of coming'; 'Now it's coming'; 'It'll be here any moment.' But the barat procession didn't appear. Chandre sent off a series of spies to find out what was happening, and each one returned with an assurance that the barat was on its way. The procession was obviously delayed because the bridegroom's party were still tanking up. It's the privilege of the bridegroom's relatives to arrive drunk, but they take it amiss if the bride's relatives have been drinking. By ten o'clock in the evening, even the laconic Chandre was becoming a little worried. He said to Kamal, 'I hope they won't arrive too much in drink, because then there could be trouble with some of the young men.' Kamal replied, 'There's nothing you can do about it. It's their occasion to make merry.'

Eventually we saw a bright light in the distance moving towards us. It seemed to move very slowly and to stop frequently. As the light got nearer, we picked up the sound of a deep baritone voice amplified by vast loudspeakers singing a hit from an old Bombay film – '*Mere sapnon ki rani, chale ao*' – 'Come, queen of my dreams.' Actually it was the raja who was coming to Chandre's Rani. The procession halted again just before rounding the last corner. Some children ran towards it, but they were called back – tradition demands that the bride's party must wait for the arrival of the procession. The music faltered, and I wondered whether everyone, including the bandsmen, was having a last pull on the bottle before entering the no-drinking area. If so, it must have been a quickie, because the music soon picked up again and the head of the procession, brightly lit by Petromax lights, rounded the corner. Chandre's generator chose this moment to give up and so we – the receiving party – were plunged into darkness.

The first thing I saw was a zoo jigging up and down vigorously. There were white storks, gaudily striped tigers, black bears, and monkeys – all made of papier mâché and cotton wool, and all held aloft by young men dancing the bhangra. The bhangra is a Punjabi dance which has now become standard at all northern Indian weddings and has deteriorated into a hybrid pop form heavily influenced by Western jiving and Indian film choreography. The Hindu gods mingled with the menagerie. There were pictures of Krishna, famed as a lover; the ever-popular monkey-god Hanuman; and Ram with his wife Sita, the hero and heroine of the epic the *Ramayan*, which was top of the television charts at the time. Even the then prime minister, Rajiv Gandhi, was numbered among the Hindu pantheon for this wedding.

Next came the singer. Miraculously, no one tripped over the wires which connected his microphone to the generator bringing up the rear of the procession. He was accompanied by bandsmen in red uniforms with flat hats and white plimsolls. There were trumpeters, clarinettists and even a sousaphone-player blowing their hearts out. Behind them came the hero of the night, Manoj, sitting on a peacock throne wearing a golden turban and garlands of currency notes round his neck. The throne was set on a converted jeep covered with bright-coloured bulbs flashing in circles, diamonds and arcs like rainbows. It looked like a gigantic jukebox. Behind the jeep came the generator, spewing out black smoke. I said to Gilly, 'Manoj looks like a Hindu god seated on a throne.'

Gilly replied, 'He's either a very bad-tempered or a petrified god.'

Manoj certainly didn't look as though he was enjoying the barat. Everyone else was. Perhaps that was the problem – maybe he was like the bridegroom who would have preferred to have stayed back for the party rather than gone off on his honeymoon. It was certainly going to be a very dull night for Manoj. When the procession came to a halt in the space in front of the basti, Manoj meekly descended from his chariot and went into the house where he was to be married. There he was tended to by his sisters. He could hear the beat of the drums and the cries of the dancers – by then we had all got swept up in the bhangra. He had to sit and think about his future with a young bride whom he didn't know at all.

Such thoughts didn't trouble Chandre – by now the proud proprietor of a show which was clearly going very well. He came up to me and said with satisfaction, 'It's a big barat, isn't it?' I replied, 'It certainly is.'

The next stage in the wedding was the evening feast. In most Indian communities the bride's party has to feed the barat before they themselves can start eating. In Chandre's biradari it was a free-for-all. Outside caterers had cooked chana (chick-peas) and potatoes, the sabzi or vegetable was loki – a kind of marrow. For a dessert there were laddoos – sweets made from gram-flour and sugar. Food was served on paper plates instead of the traditional dried leaves. Chandre did not change for dinner.

After dinner, the party started again. Fireworks added to the excitement. The air was thick with the acrid smell of biris or cheap cigarettes, the smoke from the fireworks and the fumes of the barat's generator. The members of the barat breathed the sour smell of cheap country liquor, but I saw only one young man who was obviously drunk. He was led away by his friends, presumably to rest and sober up. There was no disorderliness, no fighting.

I saw Mahipal and two other young men making their way through the chaos with charpais on their head. Sensing that they were meant for us, I went over and asked where they were going. Mahipal said he was taking the charpais to the temple on the embankment, about a quarter of a mile away, where arrangements had been made for us to sleep. I persuaded Mahipal that we would be quite happy sleeping in the courtyard, and so he took the charpais back. We went to bed under the night sky outside Chandre's house. That was a decision I was to regret.

It wasn't until the fireworks, music and dancing ended at five o'clock in the morning that I managed to get any sleep. The respite didn't last long – I was soon awakened by loud snoring. At first I thought I had been woken by my own snoring – that has happened. But then I came to my senses and realized that the offender must be someone else, because the snoring had not stopped. I looked across to the charpais where Gilly and Avrille were sleeping peacefully, with their mouths shut. Neither of them was the culprit. The snoring was unusually loud but very regular and seemed to be coming from almost under my charpai, but when I leant over the edge of the bed I could see nothing. I gave up, covered my head with my sheet and somehow managed to get to sleep again. At first light I was woken up by a young girl removing a large log of wood from a hole in the mud wall just by my charpai. There was a great deal of grunting and snuffling and a huge black sow crawled through the hole on bended knees. A long, thin snout, fangs and a comb of bristles along her back showed that the blood of a wild boar ran in her veins, so it would probably not have been a good thing if I had tried to stop her snoring. Wild or not, however, the sow had a very good relationship with the young girl, who drove her past my charpai and out towards the fields, crying 'Harrrrr, Harrrrr, Harrrrr!'

A few minutes later we were brought steel mugs full of steaming sweet tea, and Chandre's relatives enquired solicitously about the next of the day's problems – what they called 'lavatory'. I lacked the dexterity to perform my morning offices squatting in the fields and so gladly accepted the offer of the facilities in the hostel of the nearby temple. Gilly and Avrille disappeared with Chandre's sister-in-law for their ablutions, which were more thorough than mine. They had full-scale bucket-baths, dousing themselves with water from a huge brass pot while hidden from the other guests by a mud wall built as a screen to one side of the courtyard in Chandre's sister-in-law's house. My ablutions did little for my appearance, which was by now beginning to resemble Chandre's on the night before, but after their baths Avrille and Gilly looked as though they had spent the night in a luxury hotel. I waited for breakfast, while they went off to see Rani.

We had been told that the auspicious time for the wedding ceremony had been set for the early morning, but Rani had still not bathed or put on her wedding finery. She was sitting in the room beside the courtyard where the wedding was to take place, attended by her female relatives. She stared at the floor and wouldn't speak – wedding nerves had got the better of her. Eventually she admitted that she hadn't slept all night. For most of the time she had stayed inside the room, but occasionally she had gone out into the courtyard to serve water to her guests. 'Poor child,' said Chandre's sister-in-law. 'At times like this a girl should have her mother near her. We are doing what we can, but a mother is something special for 41 a girl.' As Gilly and Avrille left, they heard the sister-in-law offering motherly advice to the young bride. 'Respect your mother and father-in-law. Live with them in peace and listen to what they tell you. Look after your husband. Above all, don't fight with anyone in your new home.'

While the girls were away, Chandre came to keep me company. I asked him what he had done all night. 'Nothing,' he said with surprise. 'Come on, Chandre,' I said. 'Did you talk to people?'

'Yes,' he replied.

'What about?'

'I asked them, "Is everything all right?" They said, "Yes, it's fine." But everyone wanted to know about you. They said the best thing about the wedding was that you, my sahib, had come.'

Seeing my embarrassment and disbelief, Chandre said, 'Honestly. It's true.'

I hurriedly changed the subject to Chandre's still unkempt appearance. 'You really can't go to Rani's wedding ceremony in those clothes,' I said.

'No,' he agreed. 'I have got some new clothes. You'll be surprised when you see them, but I have still got a lot of work to do.'

'What work?' I asked. 'Surely it's nearly time for the marriage to take place. You said it would be early in the morning because that was the auspicious time.'

'Well, if we aren't ready, it can't be,' said Chandre with his customary logic.

42   'But what is this work?' I insisted.

'Well, I've got to cook your breakfast, haven't I?'

'No,' I said firmly. 'We can go without that if necessary. Why don't you go and get changed so that the marriage can start?'

But Chandre could not be budged. All I could achieve was to persuade him that he should start cooking breakfast at once.

After breakfast we hung around watching cooks kneading a mound of atta into dough for chapattis, to be baked in a tandoor or oven they had dug in the ground. This was the start of the preparations for the main feast. The members of the barat were waking up and straggling bleary-eyed into the fields for their lavatory.

We wandered around aimlessly until a miraculously transformed Chandre reappeared to take us to the ceremony. His hair was neatly brushed, he was closely shaved and he was wearing an immaculately pressed, cream silk kurta with matching trousers. I had never seen him look so smart.

The wedding took place in the small courtyard of the house where Rani was staying. We were very touched to see that she was wearing the pink sari we had given her. The edge of her sari was drawn over her face. Manoj was sitting next to her, wearing a smart suit buttoned up to the collar and a pink turban topped with a crown made of silver and gold paper covered with flowers. The couple were sitting on the ground under a conical thatch supported by three up-turned ploughs. A stick stood in the middle of this mandap or platform with mango leaves and earthen pots tied to it. Women sat in one corner of the courtyard singing songs of 43 rejoicing. Relatives filed past Manoj and Rani, touching her feet and smearing tilaks on his forehead, and putting money into a steel tray by the fire. No Brahmin priest was involved in the ceremony, but the elderly chaudhuri who had supervised the business transactions the night before squatted by the fire reciting mantras and dropping herbs into the flames.

Eventually the chaudhuri told the couple to stand up. He tied Manoj's scarf to a white cotton shawl which Rani was wearing and gave them a gentle shove towards the fire. Manoj led his bride around the flames seven times – a marriage is said to be a bond which lasts seven lifetimes. Some of the bridegroom's party let off fireworks, but this was soon stopped by the elders from Chandre's side. The couple then went inside the house to be 'worshipped' by the guests. Rani, according to tradition, should not have lifted her veil until she reached her in-laws' house, but happily for all of us she did show her pretty face, now smiling shyly. She wore a heavy gold ring through her nose, and a pendant on her forehead hung from a gold chain pinned to her parting.

Chandre had slipped out before the ceremony ended – he had received a message that the cooks were refusing to start baking the chapattis until they were given a bottle of liquor, and he had gone to find them one. He was back and waiting for us when we came out of the house after paying our respects to the couple. 'Come quickly,' he said – 'I want you to see the pigs.' There they were in the open space in front of the basti – two monsters, trussed up in the back of a three-wheeled minitruck. As they were being lowered to the ground, Chandre said to me with pride, 'One weighs more than a quintal [a hundredweight].' I was relieved that the pigs had come from outside and that my friend of the previous night was not to be sacrificed.

None of us wanted to watch the slaughter, but Chandre insisted. Mahipal came forward with a long iron spike, knelt beside the larger of the two pigs and stabbed it through the heart. Then we knew what to squeal like a pig means. After the pigs' bristles had been singed off with burning straw, Mahipal washed off the black, charred hair under the pump and started to cut the carcasses up into small pieces for the curry. The meat was cooked in huge, black metal pans, stirred with bamboo sticks.

While the guests were waiting for their feast, they were kept amused by a magic-wallah and three young men who specialized in dances appropriate for a day when fertility was very much on people's minds. Two of them were young and slim; they were dressed in saris with false breasts filling out their blouses. The third was slightly older, his teeth were stained by pan, or betel-leaf, and he looked thoroughly dissipated. He was dressed like a monkey with a large tail and a larger penis, which he used to good effect to entertain the guests and arouse the young dancers. They wiggled their hips and wobbled their false breasts seductively to the music of bagpipes – not instruments I would have associated with this sort of entertainment. Eventually one of the young 'women' fell to the ground in ecstasy and the 'monkey' leapt on top of her to shouts of approval from the audience.

We were never to know what other entertainments lay in store for the guests, because Chandre came to call us for our 45 lunch – chicken curry, which had been specially prepared for us because pork is one thing I won't eat in India.

As we had to get back to Delhi that night, Chandre excused us from waiting for the barat to move off and take Rani to her new home. The whole wedding party seemed to surround our little red van to see us off, but we eventually completed our goodbyes and were allowed to leave accompanied by our dhobi and his wife.

As we drove away, I thought how removed I had been from the wedding itself. I had been treated like royalty: the guests were honoured by my presence, but they kept their distance. I wondered whether I had been at fault – whether I should have made more effort to talk to members of the barat. Perhaps I should have stayed up all night. On many occasions I still have difficulty in knowing how to be a foreigner in India, but at the wedding I don't think it was entirely a problem of being a foreigner – I was Chandre's sahib, and the members of Chandre's biradari don't expect to be on intimate terms with their employer. Then again, the wedding was also very much an affair of Chandre's biradari, and I think that anyone from outside that tight-knit community would have felt a stranger. I have talked to Chandre about this since the wedding, and he has assured me that I did exactly what was right. I am still not sure: I would feel more comfortable if I had taken more part in the wedding, but that would have meant forcing myself on the guests, which can be just as condescending as standing slightly aloof – and incidentally a lot more embarrassing for everyone.

46   Within a year of the wedding in Molanpur, Rani had given

birth to a son in hospital in Delhi. When Chandre first saw him he burst into tears, because the baby's left foot was twisted at a right angle to his leg. Rani, more sensibly, accepted the doctor's assurance that this could be put right by six months in plaster.

When Rani returned from hospital, Gilly and Avrille took her aside and explained how putting off her next child would help her to look after herself and her baby's health, and would mean that the family would be better off. Her husband, Manoj, was unemployed. They suggested an IUD and told her it would not harm her or her baby, or prevent her having children later on. It transpired that Rani already knew all about family planning from friends and television – all she needed was some help in going about it. So the next day she went off happily with Gilly to the local Marie Stopes clinic. Manoj put up some opposition, but Rani handled him efficiently and he was won over. Unfortunately, the women of his village were not amenable to persuasion. When the baby's foot had been straightened and Rani returned to her in-laws' home, the women there insisted she have the IUD removed – they thought she had been immoral to interfere with herself.

Chandre was much exercised about getting a job for his son-in-law. Avrille sent Manoj and Rani for an interview as domestic servants for an executive of a Middle East airline. When they came back, Chandre came to me with a long face and said, 'I don't know whether I should let Rani live in the house of a habshi.' 'Habshi' means 'Negro'.

I told Chandre rather pompously that there was nothing 47

wrong with Africans, and anyhow this man was an Arab. Chandre replied, 'That's all right, but Rani says that the habshi wants her to cook beef.'

'Well, you sometimes cook buffalo here.'

'That's true. But these people, they eat too much meat.' I couldn't budge Chandre, but Rani herself overruled his objections and the couple went off to work for the airline executive. Unfortunately Manoj didn't take to domestic service – it was nothing to do with the beef, it was just that he didn't like the work – so he's now back in his village waiting for me to find him a more congenial job.

Shortly after Manoj gave up domestic service, Gilly and I returned to Molanpur. When I started to write Chandre's story, I realized that I needed to know more about his village. With Chandre as guide, we managed to get lost within a mile of the village – which didn't seem to surprise any of his biradari. It was a cool winter afternoon. There was a cloudless, bright-blue sky – the sort of sky that welcomed me when I first came to Delhi in 1965, though a foul, throat-rasping smog now characterizes winter in the Indian capital. Without a wedding to motivate it, Molanpur was looking a little shabby. The thatched roof of one of the houses had collapsed, and the paintings on the walls had faded. There were piles of dried cow-dung where we had stood to welcome the barat.

The first thing I wanted to do was to see the field from which Chandre had run away to Delhi. Chandre said he would send some chokras – young boys – with us. He never bothers to visit his own fields, which are cultivated for him by a member of the Yadav farming caste. On the outskirts of Molanpur, some Yadav farmers were crushing sugar cane to make gur or jaggery – coarse brown sugar. A pair of bullocks yoked to a shaft walked round and round in a circle. The shaft turned two drums, between which the cane was crushed. A young boy walked behind the bullocks, clicking his tongue, flicking their tails and occasionally thwacking them with a stick of sugar cane to make sure their monotonous task didn't send them to sleep. Nearby, the glutinous green juice squeezed out of the cane simmered in an open black pan at least five feet in diameter. The pan was heated by an oven dug into the ground and fuelled by crushed cane and eucalyptus leaves. Even the water used to wash out the pan after each boiling was not wasted – it was given to the cattle to drink. The farmers told me that this was the only industry in the area, and it was very much a seasonal affair. Molanpur had done quite good business in hand-sewn shoes, but the cobblers had lost out to nasty, cheap plastic products.

We crossed the bandh or embankment which protects Molanpur from the Ganges and walked towards the sacred river. The mud path was baked hard by the sun. A sea of yellow stretched away into the distance on both sides – the bright yellow of mustard and the lighter yellow of ripening wheat. The boys didn't know exactly which of the small fields belonged to Chandre, but they assured us that some of them did. Clumps of sainta grass fifteen-feet tall hid the Ganges from us. We asked the boys how far the river was, and when they said a mile or so we decided to walk on.

Indian villagers are notoriously bad measurers of distance, 49 but fortunately these boys were not too far out. When we reached the sacred river, the sun was going down behind broken clouds. It was what is known in the villages of northern India as a 'partridge-feather' sky. The setting sun cast a glittering golden band across the waters of the Ganges. The ragged banks and islands of sand testified to the river's wanderlust – the Ganges knows no boundaries. A man stood waist-deep in the water, praying with his face turned towards the fast-setting sun. It was one of those many moments when I think, 'I can never leave this country.'

As we walked back to Molanpur, villagers were returning home – on their heads, bundles of the long grass which is used for thatching and making furniture. Fires were glowing beside the tube-wells where farmers were settling down to keep watch on the pumps which would irrigate their fields throughout the night. The boys asked me to get them jobs in Delhi. I tried to persuade them that I didn't have any influence with the government, but I don't think they were convinced.

That night we again sat down inside the basti where we had waited for the wedding to start. Chandre's relatives gathered around us. Tau, who had never contributed to Rani's wedding expenses, brought out his hookah. Chandre's nephew Kamal said, 'Most of us smoke biris or cigarettes now.'

Hari Singh, the Yadav farmer who worked Chandre's land, sat on the edge of a charpai. If most of what I'd read about caste in Indian newspapers had been true, he should never have allowed himself to be seen in a Harijan basti. I had once asked Chandre how he could trust a man outside his biradari to farm his land for him – especially when that man came from a higher caste, and a caste which was notorious for brutalities against Harijans. Chandre replied, 'We went to the embankment and he swore by the baba [Hindu holy man] of the temple that he would not cheat me. I don't think he has. In fact he is a friend. When his wife was ill, he brought her to Delhi and he stayed with me while his wife was in hospital.'

I asked the Yadav what his biradari thought of this friendship with a Harijan. He said, 'In this village there are not those sort of problems. We mostly keep ourselves to ourselves, but if some work has to be done with another caste we do it. That's why I look after Ram Chandre's farming.'

It was the biradari that I really wanted to talk about. I thought that, as a younger man, Kamal might have had doubts about the system, but he said, 'It's still very important. We help each other in the biradari from birth until death. When anyone dies, one or two hundred people will collect for the funeral and will take the ashes to the Ganges. Men and women come. Only biradari people help you in times of trouble.'

Gilly asked, 'Do you ever make someone hookah pani bandh these days?' Everyone except Tau laughed, and Kamal said, 'He's the only one we could make that, because he's the only one who smokes a hookah.' 'Hookah pani bandh' means being barred from smoking the communal hookah or drinking water with members of the biradari – social ostracism. Chandre thought for some time and then said, 'Actually there was 51 a case, although it's very rare now. It was because of my cousin Ramu. Someone spoke badly about his daughter, saying she was living a dirty life. He reported it to the panchayat and they found the man had done wrong.'

'How long did the bandh last?' Gilly asked.

'I think it was about a year,' Chandre replied. 'Then he asked for forgiveness and he was made to pay a fine.'

'Can we meet the chaudhuri of the biradari?' I asked.

Kamal replied, 'Yes. That's not difficult. We'll take you to Gavvan tomorrow to see him. But I want to ask your help, Sahib. You must do something about Tau. He has had his pay cut by the government from sixty rupees to thirty each month.'

'Thirty rupees a month,' I said with surprise. 'I thought you could earn thirty rupees in two days working in the fields nowadays.'

'Yes, thirty rupees,' Kamal replied firmly. 'It's a disgrace.'

'What work do you do, Tau?' I asked.

The old man said, 'I am a sweeper.'

'Yes I know that,' I replied – 'but where?'

'In the government school on the embankment.'

Eventually I extracted the whole story from the taciturn Tau. He had been cleaning the school next to the temple for many years. He had been paid sixty rupees a month for his labours. Recently the headmaster had called him in and said that the government inspectors had instructed that he should be paid only thirty rupees. The headmaster couldn't explain this. I suggested that maybe the headmaster was pocketing the other thirty rupees himself. Tau grunted, 'It's possible.'

'How much do you sign for?' I asked.

'I don't know. I make a thumbmark.'

I turned to Kamal and said, 'Why don't you ask to see the register, so that you can see what Tau is signing for? My guess is that the headmaster is taking the money. I can't believe that, with all the money government employees get nowadays, Tau should only be paid thirty rupees a month.'

'It's very difficult for us to interfere,' Kamal said. 'If we make too much trouble, Tau will lose his job altogether. I can't go to see the master sahib. He will just say it's not my business.'

After finding out that the headmaster lived in the nearby town of Gavvan, I suggested that we might go and see him the next day. Kamal thought that was a good idea, but I wasn't entirely certain.

'Supposing the master sahib is annoyed by my visit,' I said. 'He may not say so to my face, but he may take it out on Tau when I have left.'

'That's possible,' Tau grunted again. 'Then you will have to come back.' Everyone laughed except for Tau, who did not see what was funny about such a common-sense remark.

'All right,' I agreed – 'I'll go to see the master sahib. But first of all you must show me the school you clean tomorrow.'

'I won't be cleaning it,' Tau replied – 'it's Sunday.'

'I know, but you can still show it to me.'

'I suppose so.'

On that somewhat unpromising note we left the problem 53

of Tau until the next day and started to clear up some of the questions I had about Chandre's wedding.

That night, because it was quite cold, it was decided that we should sleep inside Chandre's one-room house. Two charpais and thick razais or quilts were provided for us. A small oil-lamp was set in a niche in the wall. Just as we were going to sleep, Kamal walked through the open doorway with a cricket bat. 'What on earth is that for?' I asked.

He replied, 'To hit dogs with. They come in during the night.'

Fortunately they didn't. Nor was I woken this time by the sow.

The next morning Tau had lost interest in the whole venture, so Chandre took us to the temple on the embankment with one of his nephews. The village had woken up by the time we set off. My friend the sow had been let out. The goats had been tethered and were nibbling greedily at branches of jamun trees. Brown and white puppies were sucking at the sagging breasts of their emaciated mother. The chickens had flown down from their roosts on the thatched roofs and were scratching furiously for their breakfast. Grey babblers – known in India as 'sat-bhai' or 'seven brothers', because they are said to go around in groups of seven – were rummaging noisily in the piles of dried cow dung. The residents of the basti were returning from their ablutions. A family party was disembarking from a bullock cart outside the next-door basti, which belonged to the dhobis. They were going to the Ganges for the naming ceremony of their son.

The temple had been built in honour of a Hindu saint called Hare Baba, who had died as recently as 1971 with the words 'Hare Bol', or 'Speak the name of God', on his lips. Chandre told me with pride that the baba was credited with building the thirty-mile-long embankment to protect Molanpur and 6,999 other villages from the Ganges when it flooded. An old pilgrim told me that the baba had miraculously built the embankment in six months, because he was so moved by the plight of the villagers in a great flood in 1922. The pilgrim said, 'I remember we all had to climb into trees. We even had to defecate from the branches.' A retired official of the Uttar Pradesh Roadways who spent his time visiting the holy places of India gave us a guided tour.

The main temple was built around a courtyard. Its centrepiece was a shrine with a life-size alabaster statue of the baba sitting upright, complete with beard and black spectacles. He was wrapped in a saffron robe, had a red tilak on his forehead and was sitting upright as that was the position in which he had been buried immediately beneath the spot where his statue now stood. Hindu saints are sometimes buried, sometimes thrown uncremated into rivers. Under the shade of the tall trees outside the main temple there were smaller shrines. Monkeys climbed over the roof covering the image of the monkey-god Hanuman. A small group of women were pouring Ganges water over a lingam – a phallus, the symbol of Shiva – which a dog was licking happily. The non-stop chanting of 'Hare Bol, Hare Bol' could be heard. Chandre said, 'The chanting hasn't stopped since the baba died.'

Tau's school was about fifty yards away. It was a large 55

building with several classrooms. Pious platitudes were painted on its walls. One said, 'It is our duty to work, the fruit is in the hands of God.' If Tau could have read it, he might well have thought, 'You can say that again.' There was no way, as far as I could see, that anyone should be paid just thirty rupees a month for keeping that school clean.

Back in the village, Chandre made breakfast for us and we discussed plans for the visit to Gavvan to see the headmaster and the chaudhuri. Tau agreed to come with us, but insisted that someone else would have to do the talking. We found Maulvi Ayub Khan, the headmaster, in a small brick-built house. The master explained to me that the rates of pay were set by the basic-education official. Apparently the sweepers didn't have a union, unlike the peons or messengers, and that was why they got paid so badly. I found it hard to believe that this pious elderly man would be stealing half of Tau's meagre pay-packet, and I retreated hurriedly before any other member of our party suggested that. It would have been highly embarrassing if the villagers had said that I had made such a suggestion.

As we were walking away, Chandre proposed that we ask the chaudhuri for his help in the matter. He was sitting in the sun outside his house, surrounded by members of the biradari. When he saw me, he leapt up with remarkable agility for a man who claimed to be eighty-one and gave me a smart salute. 'I was in the army as a sweeper,' he explained. He was still wearing khaki, topped by a yellow turban whose tail almost touched the ground. He was a very small man, barely five feet tall. When Chandre introduced me, he said,

'I know you. You came to Ram Chander's wedding. You did very well for him by paying for it.'

I protested that I had made only a very small contribution, but he wouldn't hear anything of it. 'No, no. I know what you did. I said the mantras at the wedding, so I know.'

I asked him how he had learnt the mantras. He replied, 'I was taught them. You don't have to know how to read and write to learn them. Now I'm teaching my son. You see, people in our biradari like to be married by an important man, otherwise there will be no evidence that they are married.'

I didn't quite understand this, so I asked Kamal to explain. He said, 'There is no book or register it's written in, so if there's a fight later about the wedding then you have to have an important witness to say they were married.'

'Yes,' the chaudhuri said. 'There are often fights within the biradari, and it's one of my main jobs to sort them out.'

I asked the chaudhuri about the case of hookah pani bandh, and he replied, 'I can't remember a case like that for many, many years. There can't have been, because I would have given the sentence.'

I turned to Chandre, who said, 'No, there was one years ago when I was ploughing the fields.'

'You haven't done that for years, but last night you said it happened recently,' I replied.

'Maybe I did,' said Chandre. 'But now I know it was when I was still ploughing.'

The chaudhuri generously admitted that he might have forgotten the incident. With that misunderstanding cleared 57 up, we got down to talking about Tau's problem. All agreed that his wage was shameful, and most felt that there must be some brashtachar or corruption somewhere. A smart young man who spoke a little English said that he earned a thousand rupees a month as a sweeper in the municipal offices. The chaudhuri said, 'This boy is like my prime minister, because he is a reading and writing man. I am like the president, and I also have a vice-president. We are all elected, so that gives us a status. But I don't know what we can do in this case.'

'But surely you have this status so you can do sifarish [make a recommendation] to some big officer.'

'We do sometimes do sifarish to the government officers,' the chaudhuri agreed, 'but that's to get people jobs. It doesn't work always – in fact not very often. Anyhow, this seems to me like the work of a sweepers' union, and you know there are no unions in the villages.'

So we left, no further forward with Tau's case. I assured him I would take it up with the Uttar Pradesh government myself, but was not very optimistic.

When I got back to Delhi I did write to the commissioner for Uttar Pradesh, and to my surprise I got a reply: the government of Uttar Pradesh did not think the work Tau did merited more than thirty rupees a month. So much for my influence! I should never have interfered. I had done no good to Tau, and perhaps had harmed Chandre's standing in the village. He had given me such a build-up, and here I had failed on my one and only sifarish. But then probably it's only my pride which has been hurt. Chandre has, as usual, taken it all in his stride. When I next meet Tau he will, I suspect, be secretly rather pleased that his own dismal expectations were fulfilled.

PENGUIN 60s